DO YOU REALLY WANT TO VISIT NEPTUNE?

BY BRIDGET HEOS

ILLUSTRATED BY DANIELE FABBRI

amicus
illustrated

Amicus Illustrated is published by Amicus
P.O. Box 1329, Mankato, MN 56002
www.amicuspublishing.us

Library of Congress Cataloging-in-Publication Data
Heos, Bridget.
Do you really want to visit Neptune? / by Bridget
Heos; illustrated by Daniele Fabbri. — 1st ed.
p. cm. — (Do you really want to visit—?)
Audience: K-3.
Summary: "A child astronaut takes an imaginary trip to
Neptune and the outer reaches of the solar system, learns
about the harsh conditions on the planet, and decides
that Earth is a good home after all. Includes solar system
diagram, Neptune vs. Earth fact chart, and glossary"—
Provided by publisher.
Includes bibliographical references.
ISBN 978-1-60753-201-9 (library binding) —
ISBN 978-1-60753-407-5 (ebook)
1. Neptune (Planet)—Juvenile literature. 2. Neptune
(Planet)—Exploration—Juvenile literature. I. Fabbri, Daniele,
1978- ill. II. Title. III. Series: Do you really want to visit—?
QB691.H46 2014
523.48—dc23   2012025975

Editor: Rebecca Glaser
Designer: The Design Lab

Printed in the United States of America at
Corporate Graphics in North Mankato, Minnesota.

Date 102113   PO 1181

9 8 7 6 5 4 3 2

Science class is not going well. You wish you were far, far away. Like on Neptune. It's so far away you would miss grade school, middle school, and high school. Do you really want to go there?

Neptune is the farthest planet from the Sun. It will take 12 years to get there! Pack plenty to eat, including gross grown-up food. By the time you arrive, you will be a grown-up.

Also, be sure to travel in the world's toughest and most insulated spaceship. You'll soon see why.

WORLD'S Toughest Spaceship

When you finally reach Neptune, the Sun will appear as a bright star. Neptune, on the other hand, will be a giant blue ball. It's made up mainly of gas. That's why it's called a gas giant.

ONION

Methane gives it a brilliant blue hue. But the planet is mostly hydrogen and helium. There's no oxygen, so you can't breathe this air. If you exit the spacecraft, wear a space suit! Exiting the spacecraft is NOT recommended.

Storm clouds rage. On Neptune, winds blow more than 1,200 miles per hour (2,000 km/h). That's almost twice as fast as the speed of sound on Earth.

As you fly deeper into the planet, the air becomes hot and thick. So you'll want to be inside that super tough and thickly insulated spaceship!

Tough enough to withstand anything...

...except Neptune's Ocean

At last, you'll reach a slushy ocean of water, ammonia, and methane. It's a fascinating sight—that is, if it doesn't melt your spaceship. Just how tough is it?

Uh-oh. Your spaceship is, indeed, melting. Better get going!

As long as you're in the neighborhood, visit Neptune's 13 strange moons. Neptune has five thin rings and six inner moons. The moons aren't large enough to form spheres. Instead, they're lumpy and oddly shaped.

Farthest away from the planet, Nereid
revolves around Neptune in a very stretched
out ellipse. Because of its strange orbit, it may
one day collide with another moon, Halimede.

COLLISION RISKS

Triton

Triton, Neptune's largest moon, is the oddest of all. Its outer surface looks like a cantaloupe. It's a freezing −391°F (−235°C). It's not very moon-like. It's more like Pluto.

Pluto, formerly called a planet, is now called a dwarf planet. It hangs out in the Kuiper Belt. The Kuiper Belt is a ring of icy objects. Triton and Nereid may have once been objects in the Kuiper Belt.

Right now, Pluto is farther from the sun than Neptune. But for 20 years out of every 248 years, Neptune lies beyond Pluto.

You may be far from home. But you're closer to the edge of the solar system than ever. Beyond the Kuiper Belt is the Oort Cloud: a shell of icy objects at the very edge of our solar system.

You've gotten this far. You wonder what lies beyond.
What suns? What worlds? What aliens?

When you find out, be
sure to let us know!

20

ASTRONAUT Discovers WHAT
Lies Beyond NEPTUNE

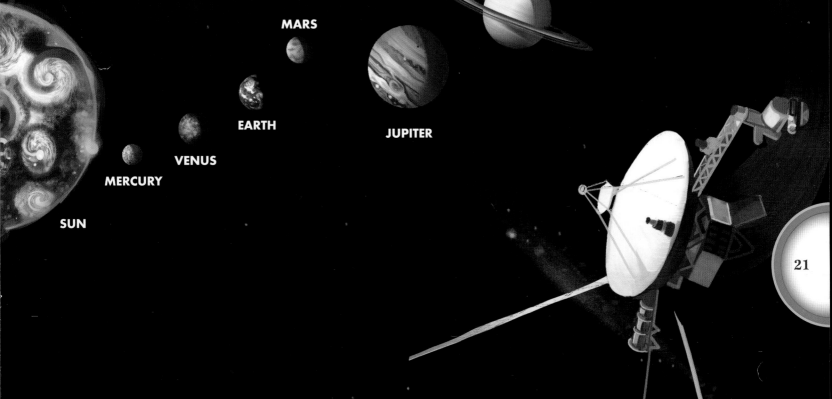

SUN
MERCURY
VENUS
EARTH
MARS
JUPITER

How Do We Know About Neptune?

We can't actually travel to Neptune. It's too far away. So how do we know about this planet? The unmanned space probe *Voyager 2* (1989) visited Neptune. It took photos and gathered data. It discovered six of Neptune's moons. It radioed the information back to Earth. The Hubble Space Telescope also took photos of Neptune.

Earth vs. Neptune

	Earth	Neptune
Position in solar system	Third from Sun	Eighth from Sun
Average distance from Sun	93 million miles (150 million km)	2,795 million miles (4,498 million km)
Year (time to orbit Sun)	365 days	164.79 Earth years
Day (sunrise to sunrise)	24 hours	16.11 Earth hours
Diameter	7,926 miles (12, 756 km)	30,776 miles (49,528 km)
Mass	1	17.15 times Earth
Air	Oxygen and nitrogen	Hydrogen, helium, and methane
Water	About 70% covered with water	Likely has water ice in the clouds and slushy water in its interior.
Moons	1	13 known moons
Windiness	Earth has a Windy City: Chicago.	Neptune could be called the Windy Planet. Its winds blow 3 times harder than Jupiter's winds and 9 times harder than Earth's.

Glossary

ammonia A chemical compound made up of nitrogen and hydrogen. It is a colorless gas. Ammonium hydroxide—ammonia in water—is used for cleaning.

dwarf planet A round body in space that orbits the Sun or another star; it is smaller than a planet.

ellipse An oval shape.

gas The form of a substance in which it expands to fill a given area.

helium A light colorless gas that does not burn. It is often used to fill balloons.

hydrogen A colorless gas that is lighter than air and catches fire easily. It can also be used to fill balloons, but it's not recommended.

Kuiper Belt A ring of icy dwarf planets and smaller icy objects surrounding the solar system.

methane A compound made of carbon and hydrogen. It is a colorless, odorless, flammable gas.

moon A body that circles around a planet.

Oort Cloud The icy bodies that make up the outer edge of the solar system, surrounding it like a shell.

orbit To travel around another body in outer space; also the path followed by a planet or moon during its orbit.

oxygen A colorless gas that humans and animals need to breathe and is essential to life.

planet A large body that revolves around a sun.

rings Bands of dust or ice particles that revolve around a planet.

Read More

Aguilar, David A. *11 Planets: A New View of the Solar System*. National Geographic, 2008.

Mist, Rosalind. *Uranus, Neptune, and the Dwarf Planets*. QEB Publishing, 2008.

Owens, L.L. *Neptune*. Child's World, 2011.

Sparrow, Giles. *The Outer Planets*. Smart Apple Media, 2012.

Websites

NASA Kids' Club
http://www.nasa.gov/audience/forkids/kidsclub/flash/
NASA Kids' Club features games, pictures, and information about astronauts and space travel.

StarChild: A Learning Center for Young Astronomers
http://starchild.gsfc.nasa.gov/docs/StarChild/
Click on Solar System to read facts about all the planets.

Voyager: The Interstellar Mission
http://voyager.jpl.nasa.gov/science/neptune.html
Learn about *Voyager 2*'s discoveries about Neptune.

Welcome to the Planets: Neptune
http://pds.jpl.nasa.gov/planets/choices/neptune1.htm
View slideshows of the best photographs taken of Neptune, plus hear captions read aloud.

About the Author

Bridget Heos is the author of more than 40 books for children and teens, including *What to Expect When You're Expecting Larvae* (2011, Lerner). She lives in Kansas City with husband Justin, sons Johnny, Richie, and J.J., plus a dog, cat, and Guinea pig. You can visit her online at www.authorbridgetheos.com.

About the Illustrator

Daniele Fabbri was born in Ravenna, Italy, in 1978. He graduated from Istituto Europeo di Design in Milan, Italy, and started his career as a cartoon animator, storyboarder, and background designer for animated series. He has worked as a freelance illustrator since 2003, collaborating with international publishers and advertising agencies.